46683410R00075

Made in the USA
Lexington, KY
30 July 2019